KU-739-829

The Hillfoots
in old picture postcards

by Ian Murray

European Library ZALTBOMMEL/THE NETHERLANDS

Acknowledgements:
Special thanks are due to David Robertson of Alloa, who also provided copies of photographs for 'Alloa in old picture postcards'.
I have also looked to the following for help or inspiration: Jim McGlone, Jenny Campbell, George Dixon, Bruce Peter, Adam Swan, Bruce Baillie, Elaine MacMillan, Billy Hunter, Helen Finlayson and the staff of the No. 5 Inn, Alva.

GB ISBN 90 288 6096 7 / CIP
© 1995 European Library – Zaltbommel/The Netherlands

Introduction

There are certain parts of Scotland – the East Neuk of Fife is one, Buchan is another and the Hillfoots a third – which have survived in local and national consciousness unaided by formal borders or administrative recognition. Of these regions some are bound together by what they contain, whether it be industry, language or customs. A second group of territories is defined by 'the other' and by their common boundary, whether the sea, the hills or the national frontier. The Hillfoots falls into this latter category.

When an area defines itself by what lies outside it sometimes does not do to enquire too closely into the ways in which its inhabitants feel themselves to be at one. If the glue of non-Englishness may sometimes seem to be the thing which holds together the diverse elements of Scottishness then what hope is there of writing a single history of the Hillfoots? Scotland has at least experienced its own single administration, the shadows of which persist to this day. The Hillfoots experience has been one of fragmented burghal and county government and the pull of different estates. The limits of this patchwork have been set by the Ochils to the north and the River Devon to the south rather than by the waxing and waning of some foreign force. The Hillfoots is thus defined as a geographical entity. Its status as an area marked off by a separate and distinctive culture in historic times is much more questionable. Despite the best efforts of such amateur lexicographers as the late Baillie James Nicol Jarvie of Alva no Hillfoots dialect has been identified which can stand comparison with that of Buchan, Fife or the Borders. The ingredients of the area's architecture, farming system and industrial history are to be found in various other parts of lowland Scotland, albeit mixed in slightly different proportions. If any distinctive and exclusive cultural identity exists in the area then it must be generated by whatever Pictish ghosts glower down from Dumyat, Castle Craig and the rock of Castle Campbell.

The location of the Hillfoots has had much to do with its failure to develop a cultural identity radically different from that of neighbouring parts of central Scotland. Well-placed to receive the shock waves from the battlefields of Stirling and the court intrigues of Edinburgh in the days of Scottish independence it has also been a thoroughfare for travellers to and from Fife and for those favouring a passage along the southern face of the Ochil Hills. Perhaps the analogy should be that of a river carrying and depositing debris along its course rather than one of a deep self-contained reservoir.

If the area has absorbed passing influences from outside then it has also drawn on its own resources to refashion itself. Whereas the fortified crags on the edge of the Ochils, the upland grazings and the lowland enclosures have all had their importance in Hillfoots history perhaps the key resource has been the fast-flowing burns which run south from the hills to the River Devon. When the textile industry began to harness the power of these burns at the end of the eighteenth century then there was an unprecedented population increase. In the fifty years from 1831 to 1881 the population of Alva grew from 1,300 to nearly 5,400, while Tillicoultry enjoyed a similar increase. Although the growth of Dollar was more modest and Menstrie's population was still less than 1,000 at the end of the 19th century all of these settlements benefited from the impetus given by water power. By the start of the 20th century whisky distilling and wood carving had come to the fore in the Menstrie area while coal mining, quarrying and brick making in the Dollar and Tillicoultry areas all clearly drew on other local resources.

The human resources of the Hillfoots should not be forgotten either. The brain power, craftsmanship and sheer brawn of skilled and unskilled workers sometimes complemented and sometimes confronted the entrepreneurial skills of Hillfoots capitalists. Although products were sent to distant corners of the world it is worth remembering that both businesses and working-class movements such as the co-operative societies continued to enjoy local control until well into the 20th century.

In the late 19th and early 20th centuries the talents of local people also found expression through a diverse range of sporting and social clubs. They were put to use by a range of religious denominations, from the breakaway United Free Church through to the Catholic Church, which had established a presence among the industrial workers in Alva. Social movements such as Temperance and political movements such as Liberalism also enjoyed much support. Although socialism was on the rise in the latter part of the period support for the Labour Party never seems to have run as deep as in the south of Clackmannanshire. When Liberalism waned the area often leant towards Independent and, later, Scottish Nationalist candidates at local level. (Dollar, with its residential rather than manufacturing bias, has tended towards the Conservative cause.) Some would see this pattern as evidence that the area has become a sliver of 'small-town Scotland' having more in common with places like Auchterarder and Kinross than with those parts of the Forth Valley where heavy industry was dominant.

As ever the Hillfoots remains open to outside influences. The local seat of administration is in Alloa but Stirling and Dunfermline are also employment magnets. The drovers and the stagecoach have now been replaced by 'travel-to-work areas'. Education and social services cut across many of the old boundaries and multi-national broadcasters and businessmen are in blissful ignorance that they ever existed. Even so, the shared experiences of people in different parts of the Hillfoots means that some spirit of independence remains. These photographs are reminders of the time when each burgh and settlement had its own strong sense of identity, stones cast up by the river that has always flowed through the area. The Hillfoots itself has often been carried along like a cork at the mercy of much greater powers, often inundated by change and yet surviving. On the journey along the river of time, from the dirt-track out into cyberspace, it has proved itself a natural traveller. These are some of the memories which it should carry to refresh itself and to open the eyes of other travellers.

The Hillfoots Road

1   The road running below the steep south face of the Ochils is the thread that has long drawn the Hillfoots towns and villages together. The main road now follows the line of the turnpike rodd of 1806 although portions of the older and higher 'back road' are still in evidence. This view of two men in a horse-drawn trap is taken from a late 19th century glass slide. In the second half of the century privately-owned transport of this kind is known to have been supplemented by the phaetons, dog-carts and gigs hired out by local hotels. Unfortunately no information survives to identify this particular vehicle and its passengers.

Blairlogie

2   The village of Blairlogie is the westernmost of the Hillfoots settlements. The present-day village dates from between 1750 and 1900 but the name appears as early as 1451, in the gift of a dowry from James II to his queen, Mary of Gueldres. In later times a square of one- and two-storey cottages was built alongside the main Stirling to Kinross road. By the middle of the 19th century Blairlogie had developed a reputation as a resort for invalids, particularly consumptives, although it was later surpassed by Airthrey and Bridge of Allan. The village was designated a Conservation Area in 1967.

The Old Castle, Blairlogie

3   This building is also known as The Blair. The main (west) portion was built by Alexander Spittal in 1543 and the east wing by Adam Spittal in 1582. It remained in the possession of the Spittal family until the end of the 18th century. After Lieut.-Col. Hare of Calder Hall took over the estate in 1891 additions were made to the north and east sides of the property.

The Old Castle, Blairlogie

Panorama from Dumyat

4   A panoramic view of Menstrie and the Hillfoots, taken from the southern slopes of Dumyat. Menstrie itself is in the foreground, with the Elmbank Mill buildings dominating the village centre. To the south-east the railway link with the main Stirling-Dunfermline line loops up towards the Distillers Company complex with its bonded warehouses. The SSHA housing at Broompark on the east of the town has yet to appear and the Hillfoots road continues through open country, beyond the houses at Dams, to Alva, nearly two miles away.

O, Alva woods are bonnie;
Tillicoultry hills are fair;
But when I think o the bonnie braes o Menstrie,
It maks ma hert aye sair

(Traditional rhyme)

Menstrie Castle

5   Two views of Menstrie Castle: the courtyard and the south side before its refurbishment. The castle started life as a plain 16th century house with turrets at its angles and crow-stepped gables, the enclosed courtyard developing later. In 1649 Robert Murray of Woodend, Perthshire sold the lands and barony of Menstrie to Major-General Sir James Holb[o]urne and in 1719 possession passed to the Abercromby family. After they moved to the new mansion of Tullibody House the castle went into decline. By the early 20th century it was being occupied by a dairyman and the outbuildings were being used as byres and cattle-sheds. It took a campaign led by the actor Moultrie Kelsall to restore the house to its former glory. The redeveloped building was opened in April 1961.

The old bridge, Menstrie

6 As the caption suggests, there appears to have been a bridge over the Menstrie Burn at this point since medieval times. The incident referred to is the flight of James III after the Battle of Sauchieburn in 1488, the culmination of six years of civil war. (Although there is a tradition that James was killed after the battle it has been suggested that he died on the battlefield. The story of his flight and subsequent assassination may well have been embellishments developed by political groupings who did not wish to be seen as having the king's blood on their hands. The reward later offered for the capture of his killers was never claimed.) Since the nineteenth century the bridge has been bypassed by the main 'Toll Road' several hundred yards downstream. The back road from Alva now finishes in a cul-de-sac on the western bank of the burn.

The Old Bridge, Menstrie.
The Bridge that James III clattered
over when fleeing from the Douglas.

The old mill, Menstrie

7   The old mill in Ochil Road, Menstrie stood by the east end of the old bridge. The building has now been demolished. The Scout Hall which now stands on the site dates from 1969. Prior to that the group had used the old malt barns, which eventually succumbed to dry rot. The house on the immediate right of the picture, now also demolished, held a set of six built-in box-beds which would have been considered sufficient even for the large families of the 19th century.

Burnside, Menstrie

8   Burnside is now known as Midtown. This late 19th century view shows the Menstrie Burn in the foreground with a wheelwright's equipment on the left bank. In the centre of the picture is Windsor Castle, now demolished. The Holburne (or Holbourne) family coat of arms, with its motto *Decum meum virtus*, which was carved on a stone panel over the door, now appears on the gable end of a present-day block of old people's housing at Midtown. There is a suggestion that Windsor Castle may have been used as a dower house after the Holburnes left Menstrie Castle. In the mid- to late-19th century this area formed the residential heart of Menstrie.

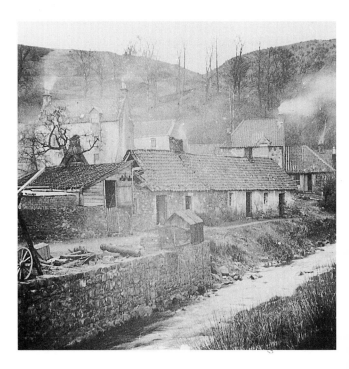

Main Street, Menstrie

9   This view, taken from the junction with Park Road, looking west, features the premises of Menstrie Co-operative Bakery & Provision Society and Menstrie Parish Church, the latter opened in 1880. (At this stage Menstrie was still in the parish of Logie.) The Co-operative Society premises contained a hall approximately 70 feet by 25 feet in size, located above the new stores. The Society had been founded in 1847 and marked its fiftieth anniversary by unveiling the two-faced Jubilee Clock which appears on this picture. The occasion was marked by a procession through the village, speeches in the Public Park and tea in the Co-operative Hall.

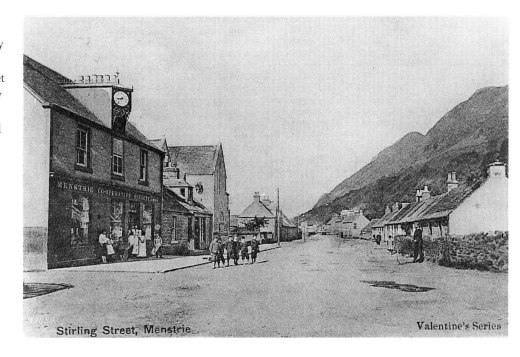

Stirling Street, Menstrie   Valentine's Series

Broomhall, by Menstrie

10   The house of Broomhall, set back from Long Row, was built in 1874 for James Johnstone, owner of Elmbank Mill. The original house, which had been used as a boys' boarding school, known as Clifford Park, was burnt down in 1940 and lay ruined for many years. In 1977 the stables were converted for housing and the former boarding school building was turned into a nursing home eleven years later. This view was taken from a postcard with a 1905 date-stamp.

Middleton Kerse

11   The house of Middleton Kerse was situated west of the Menstrie to Tullibody road in the present-day area of The Cloves. It was demolished after being taken over by the housebuilders Bett in 1965. James Meiklejohn, who built the original mansion, was an Alloa brewer who previously lived in the town's Candleriggs. The estate came into the hands of distilling magnate Alexander McNab (pictured to the side) in 1871. His firm, McNab Brothers & Co., were responsible for establishing a grain distillery at Glenochil in 1846 and for developing commercial yeast production there in the 1870s. (In 1877 they became one of the original components of Distillers Company Limited.) After his widow Ina Walls died it was sold to its last occupants, the Whitson family, in 1936. Among the peculiarities of the property was a walled garden with undersoil heating powered from the house's boiler. The building itself was reputed to be haunted by the ghost of Alexander McNab.

The Lipney

12   A view of The Lipney (or Lypney), a farm on the lower slopes of Dumyat, showing its pantiled barns. The *County Directory of Scotland* of 1894 lists one William Nicol as the occupant of the farm. Four years later the peace of the area was disturbed when the Alloa contractor Alexander Gall started building waterworks at Jerah, further up Menstrie Glen, for Clackmannan County Countil. An unlikely hamlet of wooden buildings, including men's living quarters, the contractor's office, a smiddy, a general store, a joiner's shop, a large stable and a mission station sprang up nearby.

Menstrie Victoria F.C.

13   A 1901 group picture of the Menstrie Victoria team with Menstrie Mains Farm in the background. The original team foundered but an outfit of the same name emerged to compete in the Clackmannanshire Supplementary League in the years following the Second World War.

Back row: Barry Carmichael, Bob Jackson, John Jackson, W. Thomson and Hugh Robertson.

Middle row: James Nairn, Ned Carmichael, Bob Lindsay, Bob Robertson and George Robertson.

Front: Jim Thomson.

George Robertson was later signed by Motherwell and Sheffield Wednesday and played for Scotland between 1911 und 1913.

Menstrie and Alva scholars

14   In the upper picture the Menstrie scholars of 1900 are shown posed against the wall of the old school, which had been opened in 1875 and continued in use until 1978. The headmaster at the time was William Laing (who retired in 1922) and his assistants were Misses Morrison, Whyte, Minto and Peat. In 1897 the Alva School Board agreed to allow the local Literary Association to use the premises for their evening meetings. The lower picture shows the Secondary Department of Alva Academy in 1899. The Park Place School, as it was then known, was built in 1875 on the northeast corner of Johnstone Park and subsequently extended. A separate infant school was built at Dalmore in 1886.

Myretoun House

15 Although the caption describes the house as being in Alva it lies barely half a mile from the centre of Menstrie, on the east side of the Dams Burn. It was the home of Miss Caroline Johnstone, daughter of local landowner James Johnstone. When she died in 1929 it passed to Henry James Johnstone. Alan Porteous of Alva who bought the property in 1940 was chairman and managing director of the local textile firm James Porteous & Co. (The firm operated the Meadow Mill, situated between Brook Street and the Alva Burn, until its closure in 1964.) He was also known as a leading figure in Scouting circles, having served as County Scout Commissioner.

MYRETOUN HOUSE, ALVA.

Alva Burgh relics

16   The history of Burgh of Alva spanned nearly a century from its creation as a Police Burgh in 1876 to the local government reforms of 1975. Although it never formally recorded arms the design on the left appeared on an early postcard. As can be seen it features a bag of wool, a shuttle, a distaff and a water wheel, together with the motto 'Industria et Labore', in tribute to the importance of the town's spinning and weaving industries. Alva Town Hall in Johnstone Street had been built in 1852 on a site provided by local landowner James Johnstone for a nominal amount. After its extension in 1871 it was capable of holding an audience of 800, with room for a further 200 in a lesser hall. The Cochrane Hall, which opened in 1930, usurped many of its functions and, as the picture shows, it was used as a garage before eventually being demolished.

Alva House

17   The frontage of Alva House as seen in 1904. The building apears to have developed out of a tower house dating from no later than the middle of the sixteenth century. The expanded mansion of 1636 was associated with the local Erskine family in the 17th and 18th centuries and then with the Johnstones, who added the south front and west wing around 1820. When the picture was taken the house was in the possession of Miss Carrie Johnstone. On her death in 1929 unsuccessful attempts were made to sell the property and thus to clear the debts which had built up. The apparent lack of interest in the building led on to its use for military target practice in the Second World War. When it collapsed a major piece of local (and national) heritage was lost.

The Silver Glen, Alva

18   The first silver mine was opened in 1710 by Sir John Erskine, who employed miners from Leadhills. In the space of fourteen weeks forty tons of silver worth £4,000 was brought to the surface. When Sir John was forced into exile as a result of his connections with the 1715 Rising the silver was buried in the grounds of Alva House by Lady Erskine. The promise to give the Crown 10% of the value of the diggings secured a pardon for Sir John. Both Sir Isaac Newton and Dr Justus Brandshagen from the royal silver mines in Hanover reported on the extraordinary quality of the metal. In the 1760s Lord Alva had two communion cups made from some of the remaining ore and gave them to St. Serf's Church.

SILVER GLEN, ALVA.

Beauclerc Street, Alva

19   Beauclerc Street was formerly known as Back Raw and was renamed after Lady Jemima Beauclerc, daughter of James Raymond Johnstone (1768-1830), the major local landowner. Johnstone was responsible for feuing the street in 1796. As time went by the cottages in the street were supplemented by larger houses such as Barnaigh, an 1860s mansion showing French and Italian influences, and Listerlea, a Gothicised villa built as a manse. Together with its western continuation, Back Road, it follows the line of the old road to Menstrie. In the nineteenth century Eadie's Well was to be found here.

Thomas Henderson's shop

20   A scene outside Thomas Henderson's shop in Cobden Street, Alva as captured on an old glass slide. Henderson, who died in 1903, aged 78, worked with his father in the fleshing business and then, while still a young man, spent several years as a gold digger in Australia. He later returned to work in Alva as a butcher.

Green Square, Alva

21　A crowd gathered in Green Square, Alva for the proclamation of George V in May 1910. The proclamation was read by Provost Minto in the presence of councillors and officials with the local Territorials acting as a guard of honour. (There then followed a procession along Stirling Street to the Public Park where the Town Clerk performed the same ceremony.) When the picture was taken the pantiled building on the right housed the premises of Alexander Birnie, boot- and shoemaker. The chimney in the background appears to belong to the Bridge Mill. Behind that is the Victorian mansion of Edgehill.

Stirling Street, Alva

22   A view west along Alva's main street from the bridge over the Alva Burn. The Eadie Fountain – a memorial to the Alva-born United Presbyterian theologian and scholar Dr John Eadie – and Liberal Club are in the right foreground. The bridge had been specially widened to provide room for the fountain, which was unveiled in October 1889. The Liberal Club opened in December 1901 on a site previously occupied by Perry's bakehouse. Built to a design by A.M. Lupton of Stirling, it included committee, recreation and reading rooms at the front and a large billiard room at the rear. When it first opened it had 160 members.

Wilson's Mill, Alva

23   The farmworkers pictured in front of Wilson's Mill (later known as Dalmore Works and Glentana Mills) on the west side of Alva are, from left to right: Angus McKerracher, Will Liddle, 'Bernie', Maggie Liddle and a Mrs. J. Ramsay. The firm of Wilson Bros. began to build the factory at the east end of the Toll House towards the end of 1873. Gavin Bros. of Devonside were responsible for the masonry work on the building, which was 140 feet in length and 40 feet wide. Wilson Bros., which was involved in tweed manufacture, was founded by William Primrose Wilson and James Wilson, the latter of whom lived in the Beauclerc Street mansion of Barnaigh. William Primrose Wilson lived at Manseville on Stirling Street. The mill was owned by the family firm until 1961, when it passed into the hands of McBean & Bishop.

Boll Mills and Strude Mill, Alva

24 The changing pattern of buildings and ownership over the years appears to have resulted in the Boll and Strude names being applied to a number of mill buildings in this area. The six-storey building in the background of the upper photograph was built around 1820 and has now been converted into flats. The Boll Bell which once stood atop it is now preserved at The Cochranes development to the south. The lower picture, presumably taken around the time of the First World War, shows the complex of buildings which stood to the east of the largest mill. At the turn of the century William Archibald, Son & Co. together with Ramage & Sutherland are described as tenanting and occupying parts of the Boll Mill, while another part lay empty. The manufacturers Todd & Duncan occupied the Wester Boll Mill, while the 'Upper Strude Spinning Mill' owned by James Young Mitchell had been burnt down. The Valuation Roll of the time also describes the 'Upper Strude Mill' owned by Caroline Johnstone as 'ruinous'.

Thompson's Temperance Hotel

25   Thompson's Temperance Hotel at 79 Queen Street, Alva. John Thompson, its founder, was an Englishman from Holton. Originally an apprentice moulder, he had lost his left hand, made a fresh start in the tea trade and established the hotel. He was active as a Burgh Commissioner, as a member of the Parochial Board, as a treasurer of Alva Funeral Society and was known as a quoiter and bowler. A widower, he died in July 1890 and was survived by his two daughters. Janet and Maggie Glen Thompson were still running the business at the time of the First World War.

St. Serf's Parish Church, Alva

26   St. Serf's, at the east end of modern Ochil Road, had been rebuilt in 1815 by local landowner James Johnstone to seat a congregation of 586. A sanctuary dating from 1632 formed part of the church. In 1877 twin towers were added to the Georgian building. After the Eadie Church and St. Serf's congregations merged the building was abandoned to dry rot. A fire in 1985 resulted in its demolition.

Alva Co-operative Bazaar Society

27   An orator addresses a crowd outside the premises of the Alva Co-operative Bazaar Society in Cobden Place. The society had in origins in 1845 when a group of local men, mainly weavers, rented a tiny shop from one John Henderson. For some years the enterprise traded under the name of James Wright, a local handspinner. In 1865 work began on the Cobden Place premises, incorporating offices, a committee room, a reading room and a meeting room on the first floor as well as shop premises at street level, with the laying of the foundation stone by the local laird, James Johnstone. Within the premises a double shop was allocated to groceries and provisions, while a single shop was set aside for drapery, shoes and ironmongery. In 1895 a Jubilee Clock was added to the building and the then President Thomas Leckie performed the unveiling ceremony. When the society merged with the Alva Baking Society at the end of 1910 their Johnstone Place premises (built in 1888) became part of the new organisation's assets.

Alva Parks

28   The upper of these two pictures is a view of Johnstone Park with its boating pond taken around 1910 and showing the houses of Beauclerc Street in the background. Like so many other things in Alva the park was gifted by local landowner James Johnstone. The formal presentation of the park took place in February 1856, when a procession of around 1,500 inhabitants, together with the local band, marched to Alva House and from there to the park. The Cochrane Park and Cochrane Hall, seen here behind the gates in the lower picture, were donated by the brothers James, Charles and John Cochrane, who had made their fortune as shawl manufacturers in Albany and Philadelphia. In 1923 they had bought the area that is now Cochrane Park, laying out tennis courts and a children's playground and building a pavilion and several miles of paths. The hall itself was opened in February 1930.

Alva Gas Works

29   The inauguration of the gas supply from Alloa to Alva on 18th March 1937. The picture was taken at Alva Gas Works in Henry Street by the Alloa photographer J.M. Whitehead. The plant had been bought by Alva Town Council from a private company in 1878. In 1936 it was acquired by Alloa Town Council and this picture shows Provosts Younger of Alloa and Maltman of Alva opening the valve which first brought gas from Alloa.

The Cross Keys Inn, Alva

30   This turn of the century view shows the Cross Keys Inn at 118 Stirling Street and the neighbouring Alva Printing Office. The inn was then run by Allan Watt, a locally-born spirit dealer who had originally been a cabinet maker. He owned a number of properties in the Johnstone Street and Stirling Street area and is known to have been running the Cross Keys by 1886. By 1912 J.W. Paterson had taken over as publican and within four years he had been succeeded by William Clarkson.

Hillfoots Picture Palace, Alva

31   The Hillfoots Picture Palace Theatre, two doors along from the Cross Keys in Stirling Street, was opened in September 1921. It was run by the Hudson family, who had previously shown films in the Town Hall. The new picture house, which included a balcony, could seat nearly 1,000 people. The first film to be shown was 'Madame X' and prices for performances were 1s 3d (balcony), 9d (stalls) and 5d (pit).

First aid practice

32   First aid practice at Alva in the later years of the nineteenth century. The mansion in the background is Barnaigh, with the 1873 United Presbyterian manse, now known as Listerlea, further down the hillside. Information on the early years of the local Red Cross is sketchy but a Clackmannan and Kinross branch is known to have been in existence by 1912. There was also an Alva Women's Voluntary Aid Detachment. When this was inspected by Walter Montgomery, County Director of the Red Cross, in 1915 it could then muster two Commandants, one Quartermaster, one Drill Instructor and forty rank and file members. The group had the use of six stretchers. After the First World War there was a major presentation of 600 medals to Red Cross and Voluntary Aid Detachment workers at county level. The Countess of Mar and Kellie was then president of the local branch of the Red Cross.

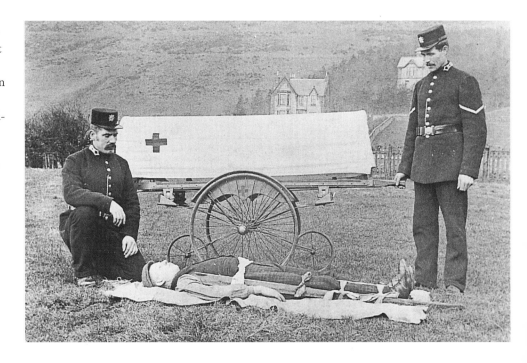

Alva Games

33 The left picture shows the Alva Games on the occasion of their fiftieth anniversary in 1895. The Johnstone Park has been turned into an oval arena ringed by a crowd which contemporaries estimated as swelling to nearly 10,000. At the top of the picture float the representations of Charles Young (far left) and John Ritchie (far right), veterans of the first Alva Games Committee of 1845. Second left is James Johnstone, ubiquitous laird of Alva and on his right the deceased William Drysdale of 'Crieff', Alva Mills. In addition to the events featured on the poster the Jubilee Games boasted shooting galleries, a switch-back railway and steam merry-go-rounds.

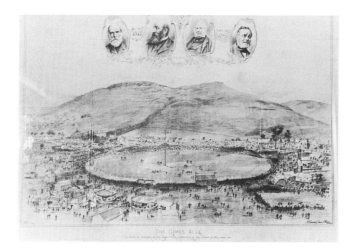

Alva Golf Club

34   In June 1900 there was a meeting of those interested in forming a golf club, chaired by the draper Atherton Gray, secretary of the Holiday Resort Association. It was proposed to create a nine-hole course, one mile 120 yards in length, at the Longbank on the north side of the town. The cost was estimated at £30. The course was inaugurated on 2nd January 1901 and a pavilion was added in May 1903. (This was replaced in 1981.) It is believed that the man on the left of this picture is James Jackson, shepherd at The Nap in the early 1900s.

Alva Cycling Club

35   Alva Cycling Club was formed in July 1891, its first captain being a Mr. T. Little and its first secretary one Thomas Callum. A newspaper report of July 1892 notes that the club had met in 'Mr Green's refreshment room' to present medals to the winners of its 2½ mile race. By 1895 the club's fixtures included runs to Tullibody, Glendevon and Bridge of Allan.

Alva Hibs F.C.

36   A team photograph taken at the time of the First World War. In 1917 the team were playing in the Clackmannanshire Amateur League. In the 1920s they played alongside Alva West End in the Clackmannanshire Secondary League and appeared in the Scottish Juvenile Cup. While Hibs appear to have played mainly in the Public Park their more illustrious neighbours Alva Albion Rangers, who fielded teams at both junior and juvenile level, got as far as building a new grandstand on the west side of Tollcross Park in 1924. According to local folkore the Rangers were assisted by a 'twelfth man', a crow which perched on their crossbar.

Alva Curlers

37   Four curlers on the pond at Dickie's Wells, south of Alva, in January 1893. In that year the president of Alva Curling Club was George Kennedy and the secretary was the local solicitor James W. Dickie. Dickie was an important figure in the Alva of his day. He acted as secretary of the local Liberal association and agent for Eugene Wason, MP, as well as being Clerk to the Gas Commissioners, secretary of the local building society and Town Chamberlain. He also owned property in the Stirling Street, Ark Street and Park Street areas of the town. The pond itself was built in 1862 by the local firm King & Penny after the club received the perpetual lease of land from local landowner James Johnstone at a nominal annual rent.

Tillicoultry Town Hall

38 The Town Hall at the top of Ochil Street started life as the Popular Institute in 1859. The campanile which was added in 1879 as a result of the generosity of local mill owner James Archibald still stands although the hall was demolished in 1986. The building was taken over by the Town Council in 1905. The organisation running it had found it a financial liability and the Town Council and their forebears, the Burgh Commissioners, had been meeting there for some time.

Old Town, Tillicoultry

39   The Old Town appears to have developed from the old village of Westerton (formerly known as Cairnton). At the time of the 1793 *Statistical Account* the parish minister of Tillicoultry was recommending the establishment of 'some public works, such as a woollen manufactory, or a cotton mill, or a printing field' at Westerton, then a collection of mainly single-storey houses. A bridge across the Devon was also advocated. By the time of the *New Statistical Account* in 1841 it was reported not only that 'there are several large and well-built mills, lately erected for the woollen manufacture' but also that there was now a 'spacious and secure' bridge over the river, as well as a foot-bridge.

Tillicoultry House

40   This view is taken from a postcard stamped 1907. The Tillicoultry estate was granted to the Mar family by Alexander III in 1261 and later owners included Sir William Alexander of Menstrie. It was bought in 1814 by R. Wardlaw Ramsay and the house pictured here was built fifteen years later. A hundred years later the building began to fall into decay. It was finally de-roofed after it was vacated by Major A.B. Wardlaw Ramsay in 1938.

Burnside, Tillicoultry

41 A postcard view of Upper Mill Street near its junction with High Street. On the left side of the burn can be seen Middleton Mill. This was built in 1836 by Robert Archibald and Sons, who had previously occupied the 1805 Middleton Mill which stood on the same site. After 1934 it was the home of the Dunedin Stationery Company, a subsidiary of the London-based papermakers Samuel Jones & Co.

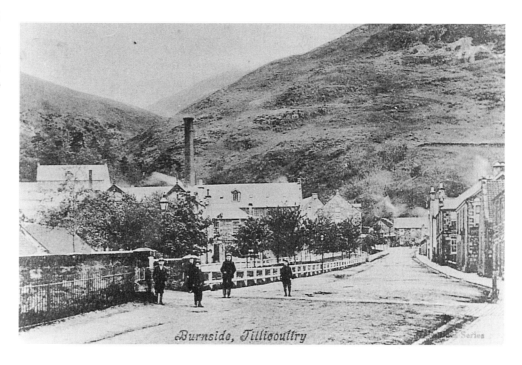

Burnside, Tillicoultry

Murray Square, Tillicoultry

42   Thomas Murray, Provost of Tillicoultry from 1928-1930 and 1936-1941 was proprietor of the local hosiery business of Drysdale, Murray & Co., having started as a worker in the firm's tweed mills. The Murray Square bus station which came into operation at the end of 1930 was one of the first in Scotland and stemmed from his census of buses. This yielded the fact that some 334 such vehicles passed through Tillicoultry in a typical day, greatly adding to traffic in the centre of the town. Murray donated a clock for the square in 1931 as well as shrubs for the rock garden. He also added an octagonal reading room, The Thomas Murray Howff for Aged Men, in 1936.

ROCK GARDENS, TILLICOULTRY

Hill Street, Tillicoultry

43   The street was laid out in 1892, with Messrs. G. & R. Cousin of Alloa being contracted to make the roadway, the kerb and the run-channels at a cost of £105 10s 7d and James Millar of Tillicoultry cementing the footpaths for £379 16s 4d. After the passing of the 1919 Housing (Scotland) Act eight council houses were built in the street as part of a programme to improve living conditions.

Ochil Street, Tillicoultry

44   A series of charabancs outside the Central Garage in the 1920s as a pensioners' outing gets under way. The Central Motor Service was run by Sylvio Bertolini of Ann Street, whose brothers, John and Fred, also ran motor bus businesses. The garage and four buses parked inside were destroyed by fire in May 1929. The street itself had been developed by the Tillicoultry Ochil United House Building Society from the 1850s onwards. By the 1870s individual properties in the area were being sold on to merchants, weavers, shoemakers and the like.

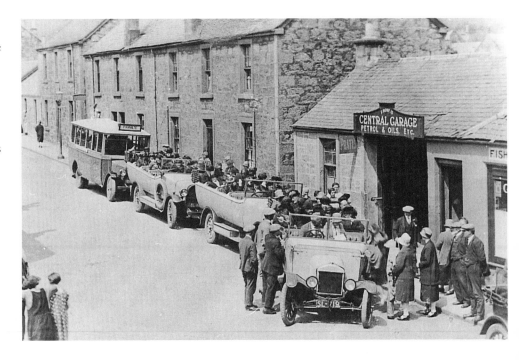

Hamilton Street, Tillicoultry

45   In 1851 one Philip Anstruther of Tillicoultry sold off seven acres of ground forming part of 'Hamilton's Park' to the Tillicoultry Ochil United House Building Society and precipitated the development of this eastern area of Tillicoultry. Hamilton Street runs parallel to Ochil Street and shares some of that street's characteristics. It has also boasted two special features, a fountain endowed by Tillicoultry Co-operative Baking Society on its jubilee in 1897, which stood at the foot of the street, and the Hamilton Street Hall. The hall is now known as the Centenary Hall, in reference to the centenary of the burgh in 1971. It was formerly owned by the local Territorials, who sold it to the British Legion in 1933.

Walker Terrace, Tillicoultry

46   Walker Terrace, Tillicoultry, at its junction with Ochil Street, looking towards Frederick Street (formerly known as Howdub). The street is named after Archibald Walker, who held local office from 1871 to 1900, as a burgh commissioner and magistrate and latterly as Provost. The street itself dates from the late nineteenth century and marks the line of the old road through the Hillfoots. Situated at the top of the afore-mentioned terraces, these detached villas are also one or two rungs higher up the social ladder.

Walker Fountain & Royal Hotel

47   One of the focal points of Tillicoultry, where High Street meets Upper and Lower Mill Street and the main road from Alva. The granite fountain was gifted by Provost Walker on his retirement in 1900. The occasion was marked by a parade from Walker Terrace via Hill Street, Ochil Street, Stirling Street and High Street to the bridge. Later there was dancing in the Public Park and a cake and wine banquet in Cargill's Crown Hotel. The Royal Hotel passed through a number of hands in the late 19th and early 20th centuries. In 1852 it was run by one Colin McColl. Gregor McGregor, who took over in the mid-1850s, appears to have made the innovation of running free transport from the hotel to meet all local trains. By 1875 George Richardson, a butler from Ratho, was being granted a public-house licence for the hotel. This side of business appears to have become more important, for by 1926 the new proprietor John MacLure was promising to furnish eight bedrooms and restore its long-abandoned residential function.

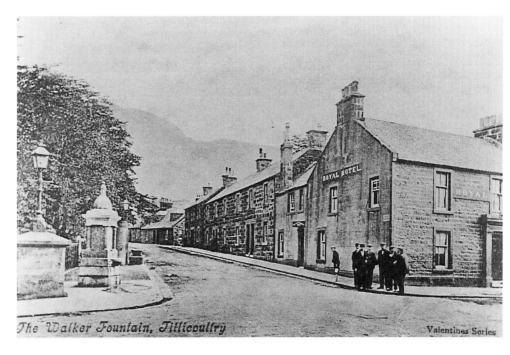

The Walker Fountain, Tillicoultry

Valentines Series

Moss Road, Tillicoultry

48   In the 19th century Moss Road was Tillicoultry's main link with Devonside, Coalsnaughton, Alloa and all points south of the River Devon. By 1874 a public meeting concerned with 'the upkeep of the Ochil Turnpike Road from Carsebridge to Tillicoultry' appointed two men to raise £100 from local householders in order to prevent the building of a toll-bar on Moss Road. The money raised delayed the establishment of a toll only until July 1877, when Richard Law was appointed to collect tolls from 6.00 am to 6.00 pm. Reports soon followed that the proprietor of Devonvale had made a road through his own grounds to bypass the toll and that carts from Alloa had begun crossing the Devon via Marchglen. By the end of September toll collection stopped after local merchants and manufacturers subscribed £250 to cover its abolition. Tolls throughout Scotland were finally abolished in May 1879 and their demise marked by shots fired from toll-house windows.

Tillicoultry Co-op chemist's

49   The Drug Department of the Tillicoultry Co-operative Society was located at 83 High Street (on the corner with Institution Place). The Co-operative Society was founded in 1839 and merged with the Tillicoultry Baking Company in 1905. The enlarged society had a number of specialised premises in the town, including a Drapery Department at 84 High Street. At the time of the merger the society had some seventy employees at these branches. The building shown was later taken over for use as the local library but has since been demolished.

The Tillicoultry flood

50   The Tillicoultry flood of 28th August 1877 took place when the mosses on top of the Ochils became saturated after a torrential and phenomenal downpour. Although Dollar and Alloa were both affected it was only Tillicoultry which experienced loss of life. The casualties here were the mill owner William Hutchison and a factory girl, Isabella Miller, both swept away with the bridge across Tillicoultry Burn which connected the two parts of Hutchison's Castle Mill. After the flood the roadways on both sides of the burn from the Heid o Toun Brig to the Middle o Toun Brig were found to have disappeared along with parts of bankside factory premises and a complete weaving shed. In the centre of the town ripped-up cobbles were to be seen mingled with other debris as the waters receded.

Devonvale Mills

51 A view which appeared in Samuel Jones & Co.'s *Quarterly Magazine* of March 1928. The company's paper-making plant occupies centre stage but on the top left can be seen the Tillicoultry to Dollar railway line while the River Devon winds across the top right of the picture. Samuel Jones took over J. & R. Archibald's mill in 1921. Woollens production has ceased there in the early years of the century and it had been used as a barracks during the First World War. Although the original mill was built by the Archibalds in 1846 it was greatly expanded around 1870. After Samuel Jones took over they built a number of white-painted red-roofed houses in Moss Road for their employees and added the Devonvale Hall in 1936. Paper-making finally ceased in 1972, by which time the factory had passed into the hands of Wiggins Teape.

The 'Tribune' office

52   The office of the *Devon Valley Tribune* in Tillicoultry's High Street, circa 1930. William M. Bett was a native of Kingskettle in Fife who learned the printing trade in the Ochil Street office of Andrew Roxburgh's *Tillicoultry News*, which flourished between 1879 and 1900. After supplementing his experience at various printing offices in Glasgow he returned to Tillicoultry to found the *Tribune* at the turn of the century. After he died in 1934 his son Arthur Bett took over the running of the paper and was still in charge when the last issue appeared in March 1967. He continued as a printer until 1970, when his works were taken over by Ian Cooper of Alloa and Ian Reid of Tillicoultry.

Tillicoultry Merchants' excursion

53   The Tillicoultry Merchants' Association was formed in November 1918. Its first president was Andrew Roger and the secretary and treasurer Mr. A. Stewart. Other members of the committee were A.T. Brydie, J.S. Waddell and Robert Ferguson. This picture was taken on 3rd June 1919 in Ardlui. The shops in Tillicoultry had closed that day and at 8.00 in the morning two charabancs supplied by Messrs. Taylor & Son of Bannockburn left the town on a run which took them through Port of Menteith, Drymen and Balloch to Ardlui, where lunch was had in the hotel. In the afternoon the buses moved on through Glen Falloch and Crianlarich to Callander, where the party stopped for tea in the Dreadnought Hotel. The evening journey was made via Dunblane and Bridge of Allan and the charabanc returned to Tillicoultry at 10.15.

Tillicoultry Parish Church

54 The inset of the Reverend James Thomas Hall, from County Cavan, appears to date this photograph at between 1919 and 1922, the years of his ministry. The first mention of a church at Tillicoultry appears in an 1199 charter of William the Lion in which he grants it to Cambuskenneth Abbey. The modern St. Serf's Church was designed by the architect William Stirling and built in the years 1827-1829. The previous church had been built in 1773.

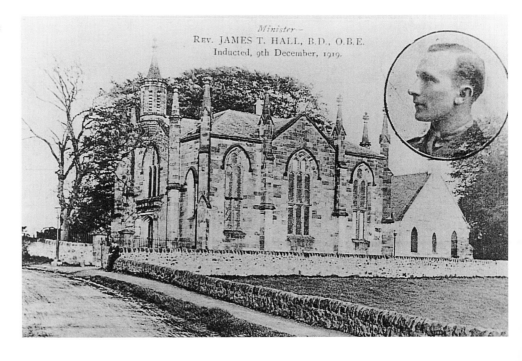

Minister –
Rev. JAMES T. HALL, B.D., O.B.E.
Inducted, 9th December, 1919.

Tillicoultry scholars

55   Primary Two of Tilli-coultry School in 1919. At this time the school headmaster was W.D. Robieson of Coalsnaughton. Peter Caproni of Ochil Street, whose photo this is, stands furthest left on the back row. The teacher is a Miss Nicholson. The old school dated from the early days of the School Boards of the 1870s and was burned to the ground in 1940. Its successor had come into operation in 1938.

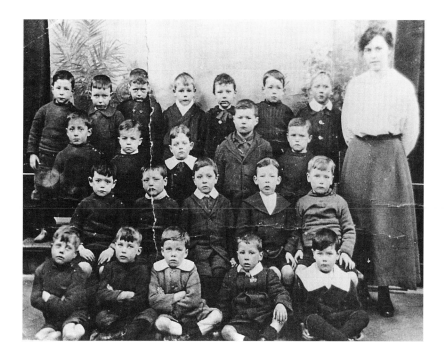

Crown Hotel Garage, Tillicoultry

56   This view of the Crown Hotel Garage, taken around 1925, shows the proprietor Charles Singer alongside what was apparently the first petrol pump in the county. The garage sold motor cycles, push bikes and accessories and repaired both kinds of bikes. Singer attained further local celebrity by arranging for a powerful radio to be set up in the garage so that the general public could listen to live coverage of the Grand National. The adjacent Crown Hotel was under the management of Charles Fraser in 1925 and appears to have been linked to the Knox brewers of Cambus, a counter to Archibald Arrol & Sons' interest in the Royal Hotel.

Tillicoultry railway & tennis courts

57   Although only the bowling green with its small clubhouse sat here at the turn of the century, tennis, football and cricket pavilions were all in operation between the wars. The *Devon Valley Tribune* records that a new pavilion was opened at the tennis courts in Tillicoultry in April 1923. As can be seen from the photograph the Devon Valley railway line was used not just for passenger traffic but also for exporting such products as coal hewn in the mines at Dollar and Tillicoultry. The picture appears to have been taken from the vantage point of the old Tillicoultry Station on the west side of Moss Road.

Tillicoultry Bowling Club

58   The club was founded in 1852. In 1908 a new club-house was opened by Mrs. Archibald of Beechwood. This photograph appeared in Samuel Jones & Co.'s *Quarterly Magazine* of 1932, at which time the club's president was James H. Young and the secretary one James Y. Liddle. Comparison with the previous picture shows that the club-house has been extended. The club enjoyed something of a renaissance in the 1920s and emulated its feat of the 1900s by winning the Balfour Trophy five times in ten years.

Ladywell Gym Club

59   A picture taken in the early 1930s. Bill Sinclair is standing, Jock Wilson is doing the backstand and William Liddell the handstand. The club was founded in 1926 and flourished in the late 1920s and early 1930s. By 1929 it had its own gym and was performing not only at local events such as the Tillicoultry Games but also as far afield as Comrie and Dumbarton and at the Scottish National amateur boxing tournament in Glasgow.

Harviestoun Castle

60   The castle was built by Craufurd Tait in 1804 on a site originally known as Easter Tillicoultry. To the west of the Harvistoun Burn lay Ellistoun and to the east Harviestoun. The latter hamlet was visited by Robert Burns in 1787 as a result of his acquaintance with Craufurd Tait in Ayrshire. Tait's cousin, Charlotte Hamilton, was the inspiration for his song 'How pleasant the banks of the clear winding Devon'. After Tait lost a great deal of money on agricultural experimentation he was forced to surrender the estate to the Globe Insurance Company in 1832. It was only in 1859 that the company managed to sell the estate to Sir Andrew Orr, ex-Lord Provost of Glasgow, who added the tower, porch and East and West Lodges. By the late 20th century the castle was once again unwanted and it was blown up in 1973.

Harviestoun Castle, Dollar

Castle Campbell

61   The upper photograph shows the castle and its bleak hinterland. To the left runs the Burn of Sorrow and to the right the Burn of Care. Control of the castle passed from the original occupants, the Stewarts, to the Campbells by marriage and towards the end of the fifteenth century the then Castle Gloume had its name changed by act of the Scots Parliament to Castle Campbell, a reflection of the Scottish politics of the time. Around 1600 the castle was improved by the addition of the East Range with its segmented arched loggia but it subsequently suffered a number of vicissitudes. The harrying of the lands of Dollar by the Macleans of Montrose's army in 1645 was followed by the burning of the castle by anti-Cromwellian forces in 1654. By the early 19th century the structure was in ruins and it only began to be repaired by Sir James Orr in the 1870s. In 1950 it passed from its then owner Ernest Kerr to the National Trust for Scotland.

Burnside, Dollar

62   This view of East Burnside in Dollar features the burgh seal with its representation of Castle Campbell and its Latinised motto 'The pleasant seat of learning'. The seal had been created in 1893, two years after the first meeting of the new Dollar Burgh Council. The first Chief Magistrate was the local chemist James B. Henderson, who acquired the title of Provost two years later. This picture shows the spire of the United Presbyterian Church (on the left) and the battlemented tower of the Church of Scotland (set back from the houses of East Bridge Street) designed by Sir William Tite in 1841.

Manor House, Dollar

63 This house in the Upper Mains area of Dollar was associated with a family of Williamsons from Dumfriesshire who first occupied it in the 18th century. It appears that the first of these, Alexander Williamson, may have inherited the house through his wife, Christian Robertson. Later occupants included David Kier, David Lambert, the Allans of Dollarbank and Glendevon Castle and Laird Izat. At one time the Dollar Academy grounds, known as Williamson's Parks, formed part of the property. It was somewhat ironic that when the house itself was demolished in 1966 its site should then be swallowed up by the Academy to provide space for a dining hall and swimming pool.

Old Town, Dollar

64   A view of the Cross Keys from Argyll Street which appeared in the 1910 *Dollar Magazine*. Hillfoot Street is directly ahead. Castle Terrace (formerly North Bridge Street) and High Street join this crossroads from the left and right of the picture respectively. This part of Dollar was on the main Hillfoots road before the building of the new turnpike route in 1806. The inn at the Cross Keys was eventually demolished in 1936.

Bridge Street, Dollar

65   Bridge Street was formed in 1806 as part of the new Ochils turnpike road. This view from the South Bridge shows the Castle Campbell Hotel on the left and William Gibb & Son's Emporium on the right. Bridge Street was also home to Muckersie's, newsagents, stationers and postcard printers and successors to Thomas Bradshaw, producer of a Victorian guide to the area. The Castle Campbell Hotel had previously been known as Robertson's Inn, and before that as Henderson's Inn. In this view the telegraph pole which stood by the south parapet of the bridge in the early years of the century has yet to appear as have the lamp-posts which stood outside the hotel and the emporium.

Brown's Shop, Dollar

66   This picture appeared in the *Borough pocket guide to Alloa, Alva, Dollar and Tillicoultry*, compiled around 1910. The shop was located in Bridge Street appears to have been associated with a Miss N.A. Brown and a Mrs. Bennett. At this time it sold millinery, flowers, straws, ribbons, silks, hosiery, gloves, laces, costumes, skirts, jackets, mantles and baby-linen. The shop is also listed in the 1916 *Almanack* produced by the *Alloa Circular* newspaper.

United Free Church, Dollar

67   An early 20th century view of West (previously South) Bridge Street and the United Free Church. The church had its roots in the 1843 secession over the issue of patronage. The first place of worship for the seceding congregation was at Shelterhall, halfway between Muckhart and Dollar. By the 1850s the Dollar element in the congregation had become strong enough to justify the building of the West Bridge Street church. As the new congregation waxed so the old church at Shelterhall waned and when the building was demolished in 1864 the stone was used to enlarge the Bridge Street structure. The 1860s Ordnance Survey map shows a toll bar on the street immediately to the west of Ochilton Road, the approximate vantage point of this photograph.

Dollar Fair

68   The genesis of the Dollar Fair can be dated to 1686 when the Earl of Perth was granted the right to hold a June and an October fair, as well as a weekly market, in Dollar. In the 20th century Dollar Fair moved to Bridge Street and the Market Park from its former stance in the High Street of the Old Town. Although four fairs were now allowed per year it was the autumn, and then particularly the spring, fairs which came to predominate. In its latter years the fair was held at the Lower Mains. This picture appears to have been taken in its Bridge Street phase, around 1906.

Waddell the butcher's van

69   Robert Waddell was born on Muirhall Farm, Larbert and arrived in Dollar in 1904. His butcher's business, which operated from premises in Bridge Street, faced competition from such as Tillicoultry Co-operative Society, which in June 1908 resolved to start a van to supply its members in Dollar, Sheardale and Coalsnaughton with all kinds of butcher meat. Waddell was also the tenant farmer of Middlehall and Allaleckie and, as such, a breeder of sheep and cattle. He regularly judged livestock at cattle shows across central Scotland. From his early days in Dollar he had been a member of the town council and in 1937 he was elected to the Provost's chair. Among his outside interests were cycling and curling. When he died in 1939 his coffin was conveyed in a hay cart lined with flowers and drawn by his favourite horse.

Dollar Academy

70 The main Dollar Academy building was designed by William Playfair in the years 1818 to 1820 in fulfilment of the will of John McNabb. McNabb had begun life as a herd boy in Dollar and had risen to become a sea captain in London. When he died in 1802 he had left half his fortune for 'the endowment of a charity or school for the poor of the parish of Dollar'. Later additions included the 1866 wing at the rear, the 1910 Science and Domestic Building and the 1937 Preparatory School. In the lower picture, taken in the early years of the century, we see a distant view of the main façade from Mylne Avenue. In the 20th century the school has enjoyed mixed fortunes. In 1922 it became insolvent and the Governors applied to be taken over by Clackmannan County Education Committee. After 1975 the school regained its independence and a new Trust Scheme was drawn up in 1981.

Dollar Institution from West Approach.

Opening of Dollar Station

71   Dollar Station stood on the so-called Devon Valley line, which ran from Alloa, through Tillicoultry, to Kinross. The section from Tillicoultry to Dollar was opened by the 11.15 am train from Alloa on the morning of Saturday, 1st May 1869. (The section of the line from Dollar to Rumbling Bridge was not completed until March 1871.) The driver of the first train out of the new station, which stood at the south end of Station Road, was Matthew Biggar and the vehicle was a 'Sharp' type locomotive. The first stationmaster was a Mr. McNess, shown here in the inset to the photograph. The first timetable for the new service offered five trains a day running in each direction between Dollar and the two main Scottish cities. The station finally closed to passengers in 1964 although freight services kept running for another nine years.

Dollar Tennis Club

72   A picture which appeared in the 1922 *Dollar Magazine*. Dollar Lawn Tennis Club was founded in 1886. Around the turn of the century the annual subscription was 27s., while croquet members paid 5s. By the time that the new tennis courts were opened in January 1913 the club had around eighty members. The *Alloa Journal* records that the opening speech was made by the then Honorary President, James Simpson of Mawcarse, who was introduced by the Secretary, Mr J. Gray Gibson.

Dollarbeg

73   Dollarbeg is a red sandstone baronial mansion which was designed by Ebenezer Simpson around 1900 for William Henry Dobie, then an important player in the tobacco industry. Previous owners of the lands of Dollarbeg had included the Abbey of Dunfermline, John Macnab, WS (around 1800) and Craufurd Tait of Harviestoun. The house was bought by the Workers' Travel Association in the 1920s for use as a hotel and this photograph appears to show the house around that time. The building continued to be run by the W.T.A. until the 1970s although it also housed an anti-aircraft battery during the Second World War.

Cowden House

74 Cowden House, which formerly stood at Castleton, south-west of Muckhart. It is recorded that there was a fortified palace here, built by William Lamberton, Bishop of St. Andrews, around 1320. Although the house shown here was not built until 1834 there had always been some form of mansion on the site in the intervening years. It was only in 1865 that the estate was bought by John Christie and the house name changed from Castleton to Cowden House. After his daughters Ella and Alice inherited the estate in the early 1900s, Ella, who travelled worldwide, set about creating a Japanese garden. The site was laid out by a member of the Royal School of Garden Design in Nagoya and the grounds cared for by a series of Japanese gardeners, the last of whom died in Muckhart in 1936. The house itself was demolished in 1952.

COWDEN HOUSE, DOLLAR.

Muckhart

75   A view of Pool of Muckhart taken from a postcard with a 1944 date-stamp. This view shows the main street with the Ochil Tea Rooms and its adjacent petrol pump. This site is now occupied by the village shop and post office. Transport links have played a major role in sustaining a community here. In early modern times the drove road to the Highlands via Glendevon was of importance. After 1813 the turnpike road from Dunfermline was extended through Yetts o Muckhart and Rumbling Bridge to form a through route to Crieff. The road from Glasgow to Perth, frequented by stage coaches, crossed this road at the Yetts Inn (now Ellaslea). Today even the country buses appear to have been superseded by private cars as the village is increasingly thought of as a desirable home for commuters.

Muckhart Mill

76   A view of Muckhart Mill taken from the 1905 *Dollar Magazine*. The mill stands on the north side of the River Devon, two miles east of Dollar. There has been a building of some sort here since the days of the 14th century grain mill powered by the Hole Burn. Around the middle of the 16th century the mill was sold by the Douglasses of Loch Leven to James Paton, at one time Rector of Muckhart and then Bishop of Dunkeld. The existing mill dates from 1666 and comprises three different rubble pantiled buildings. The cast-iron overshot waterwheel has a diameter of twenty feet and is one of the largest in Scotland. Within the last quarter of a century the mill has functioned as a children's hotel although it is now a private residence.